The Clancy Brothers and Tommy Makem Song Book

OAK PUBLICATIONS

Order No. OK 61085
US International Standard Book Number: 0.8256.0102.9

Exclusive Distributors:
Music Sales Corporation
257 Park Avenue South, New York, NY 10010 USA
Music Sales Limited
8/9 Frith Street, London W1V 5TZ England
Music Sales Pty. Limited
120 Rothschild Street, Rosebery, Sydney, NSW 2018, Australia

Printed in the United States of America by
Vicks Lithograph and Printing Corporation

CONTENTS

Foreword	5
About Our Songs	7
A Big Ship Sailing	19
A Man of Double Deed	35
Ahem, Ahem	57
Ballinderry	20
Barnyards of Delgaty	38
Bold O'Donahue	34
Bonny Charlie	63
Brennan on the Moor	46
Carrickfergus	62
Cobbler, The	55
Courtin' in the Kitchen	22
Fare Thee Well Enniskillen	58
Gallant Forty Twa, The	60
Haul Away, Joe	36
I Know Who Is Sick	47
I'll Tell My Ma	12
Irish Rover	39
Johnny McEldoo	10
Johnny Todd	51
Johnson's Motor Car	21
Jug of Punch, The	53
Jug of This	41
Juice of the Barley, The	52
Kelly the Boy From Killane	26
Kevin Barry	44
Leaving of Liverpool	54
Legion of the Rearguard	49
Lewis Bridal Song (Mairi's Wedding)	42
Mermaid, The	50
Moonshiner, The	27
Mountain Dew	28
Mr. Johnny Lad	14
October Winds	43
Old Orange Flute, The	30
Old Woman From Wexford	18
Parting Glass, The	64
Portlairge	32
Reilly's Daughter	37
Rising of the Moon, The	9
Rosin the Bow	24
Rothsea - o	40
Row, Bullies, Row	61
Shoals of Herring	59
Singin' Bird	48
South Australia	23
Tim Finnegan's Wake	33
Valley of Knockanure, The	56
When I Was Single	16
Wild Colonial Boy, The	13
Will You Go, Lassie, Go?	17
Work of the Weavers, The	45
Young Roddy M'Corley	15

FOREWORD

The collection of songs contained in this book are taken from the repertoire of just a few of the songs sung by the Clancy Brothers and Tommy Makem. It has been a difficult job to make this selection because of the great number of songs they sing, all of which have been a delight and musical experience to those who have enjoyed listening to this Irish quartet. Since the Clancy Brothers and Tommy Makem started to work "professionally" about three-and-a-half years ago, they have made a significant contribution to our musical world. Their appearances on television, on the concert stage, and in the nightclubs have won them critical acclaim not only for their musical ability, but because of their warm personality and Irish charm that has brought them a large audience of devoted followers from all sections of our country. With the growing interest of folk music in America today, the boys remain true to the musical integrity of their material. They sing their songs without commercial "distortion," adding the zest and feeling from whence their songs came. They may have taken some liberties in adaptation and rearrangements, but this has been done in good taste and in the "folk song process."

Perhaps to best describe the work of the Clancy Brothers and Tommy Makem, we can quote the comments of Robert Shelton, folk music reviewer of the New York Times: "What a pleasure to hear a folk music group that is steeped in its natural culture and oral tradition. This was part, if only part...(of)...what made the concert a memorable one... The Clancy-Makem group destroys the canard that ethnic music must always be rough, remote or of a limited appeal... They are still, however, singing the music of their past and they are doing it with understanding, passion, and charm. Most American 'mainstream' folk music groups seem wan and one-dimensional in comparison...they (the Clancys) perform with conviction and musical skill."

PAT CLANCY was born in Carrick-on-Suir, County Tipperary, one of a family of nine. During the war, he was a flight engineer in the R.A.F., serving in North India and Burma. Lest the latter sound less chauvinistic than that usually applied to an Irishman, Pat also served as an active member of the I.R.A. After being, "on again, off again, Finnegan," as far as the money department went (more often that he cared to remember), Pat first hit pay dirt in 1956 when he formed the now very successful Tradition Records. As spokesman for the group, Pat is an astute student of Irish literature, and is easily recognizable by his dark Irish good looks.

TOM CLANCY — Though his first public appearance was as a band singer in Ireland, Tom Clancy's main background has been that of an actor. Tom's acting credits, were they to be listed in their entirety, would stretch from "thar to thar". To list but a few: Tom has appeared with Orson Welles in "King Lear," Siobhan McKenna "St. Joan," Helen Hayes in "A Touch of the Poet," and Shirley Booth and Melvyn Douglas in "June." All told, including every major television dramatic program, Tom has participated in over 150 acting roles. Like brother Pat, Tom has served in the I.R.A. as well as being an officer in the R.A.F., seeing action in Europe and North Africa. A fine student of Shakespeare, Tom is the secretary-treasurer of the group; on his head falls the task of handling the many money matters that beset a group of four people as they travel from coast to coast.

LIAM CLANCY is the youngest of the Clancy Brothers. Born in 1935, Liam, like brother Tom, had his indoctrination in the theatre. While working as an insurance salesman for his father's firm, he studied acting at the National College of Arts in Dublin. It was here that he also became interested in folk songs, and he started to collect folk music throughout Ireland and Scotland before coming to the United States in 1956. He started acting professionally in 1957 at the Poets' Theater in Cambridge, Massachusetts, in a series of Yeats plays. To his credit, in the next four years, he appeared in every major dramatic television program and topped it all by appearing with Julie Harris in "Little Moon of Alban" on Broadway.

TOMMY MAKEM was born in Keady, County Armagh, into a family of musical performers. His mother was a well-known folk singer, his father a traditional fiddler, piper and drummer, and his three sisters and brother Jack (from whom he learned to play the tin whistle) followed the lead of the parents and also sung and played the musical instruments of their native Ireland. In 1955, Tommy Makem left Ireland to come to the United States; in March of 1956, he first appeared as a folksinger at a midnight concert in the Circle in the Square. He also appeared in "Guests of the Nation." He has innumerable folk-song concerts and radio shows to his credit, as well as a long list of plays in which he has acted.

ABOUT OUR SONGS

People have a way of singing about the things they do, and, as people in Ireland have been in the throes of rebellion every generation for hundreds of years, there are numerous Irish rebel songs. Some were written by men of letters, other are annonymous; all were the work of rebels — sometimes active rebels. These songs were, and still are, universally known and sung all over Ireland, although to sing or even whistle some of them was a punishable offense up to 1922 and later.

The Earl of Pembroke (Strongbow) led the first English army into Ireland in 1169. Soon English (Norman) settlements were established and for centuries there were endless raids, skirmishes, and wars. Through all these there was no united Irish effort, and not until Wolfe Tone founded the Society of United Irishmen in 1791 was Irish nationalism, as we know it, established. Under Tone's leadership, Irish and Anglo-Irish, Catholic and Protestant were united in a demand for independence form the British crown. This led to the great risings of 1798. These risings, however, were largely local and isolated, and, when expected French help did not arrive, the revolt failed. Only in Wexford was there any success.

Most of our songs are of this period. They helped breathe life into the Young Ireland movement in the 1840s and '50s and the Fenian Brotherhood in the 1860s. These songs were part of a powerful movement and were (and are) as familiar to the Irish people as household words. Sometimes they refer to actual events, such as risings and hangings, sometimes to heroes or the enemy. They may be rallying cries or laments, bitter or sarcastic or full of the spirit of savage resistance and defiance.

Irish songs are not all a reaction against England. There was a wealth of Irish culture in existence when Buckingham Palace was still a mud cabin. Going from the East to the West Coast of Ireland is like going backwards in time. The models in Dublin's Grafton Street windows near Paris fashions while the Aran Island fishermen are wearing homespuns. The songs, too, change their character. Songs like "Finnegan's Wake" and "Mick McGuire" are Dublin Music Hall songs fashioned after their London forerunners. The Gaelic songs of the West come from a much more ancient Celtic tradition. This all started with Oliver Cromwell when he landed in Ireland with his conquering army. "To hell or to Connaught" was his slogan as he drove the Celts (and, with them, their culture) back to the rocks of Connemara. There they remained, protected, at least for a while, by the barrier of language. Thank God, the Irish Folklore Commission taped a tremendous amount of the remnants of this oral culture before radio and TV dealt their deathblow.

We don't know if most Irishmen realize how thankful they should be to Mother England. We know four of them who do, Tommy Makem and The Clancys. We make a nice living out of singing Irish rebel songs, drinking songs, and laments of one sort or another. Without England on our backs, they would never have been made. The rebel songs, of course, come from a 700-year struggle to shake off John Bull's benevolence, the laments from all the times we were beaten down, and, needless to say, a drink is always needed to raise the heart in troubled times. I suppose, too, we're fortunate to be speaking English. The patrons of the folk music coffee clubs might not be too happy with a night of Gaelic. It's an ill wind that blows no good.
"Proudly the note of the trumpet is sounding,
Proudly the war cries arise on the gale..."

George Cruikshank

THE RISING OF THE MOON

The term "the rising of the moon" became synonymous with rebellion.

2. Oi then tell me Sean O'Farrell
    Where the gathering is to be
    In the old spot by the river
    Right well known to you and me
    One more word for signal token
    Whistle up the marching tune.
    With your pike upon your shoulder
    By The Rising Of The Moon.

Refrain: By The Rising Of The Moon,
    By The Rising Of The Moon,
    With your pike upon your shoulder,
    By The Rising Of The Moon.

3. Out of many a mud wall cabin
    Eyes were watching thru the night,
    Many a manly heart was throbbing
    For the coming morning light
    Murmers ran along the valley
    Like the banshees lonely croon
    And a thousand pikes were flashing
    By The Rising Of The Moon.

Refrain: By The Rising Of The Moon,
    By The Rising Of The Moon,
    And a thousand pikes were
        flashing
    By The Rising Of The Moon,

4. There beside the singing river
    That dark mass of men were seen
    Far above their shining weapons
        hung
    Their own beloved green
    Death to every foe and traitor
    Forward strike the marching tune
    And hurrah me boys for freedom
    Tis The Rising Of The Moon.

Refrain: Tis The Rising Of The Moon,
    Tis The Rising Of The Moon,
    And hurrah me boys for
        freedom,
    Tis The Rising Of The Moon.

JOHNNY McELDOO

New Words, Arranged and Adapted by TOMMY MAKEM. © Copyright 1961. 1963 by TIPARM Music Publishers, Inc. International
Copyright Secured. All Rights Reserved. Printed in U.S.A.

Try to speed up this one at the end.

Brightly

1. There was John - ny Mc-El - doo and Mc - Gee and me and a

coup-le or two or three went on a spree one day. We

had a bob or two which we knew how to blew and the

beer and whis - key flew and we all felt gay. We

vis - it - ed Mc - Cann's, Mc - Ill - mann's Hump - ty Dan's. We

then went in - to Swann's our stom - achs for to pack. We

or - dered out a feed which in - deed we did need and we

fin - ished it with speed but we still felt slack.

2.   Johnny McEldoo turned red, white and blue
     When a plate of Irish stew he soon put out of sight
     He shouted out "Encore" with a roar for some more
     That he never felt before such a keen appetite.
     He ordered eggs and ham, bread and jam, what a cram!
     But him we couldn't ram though we tried our level best
     For everything we brought, cold or hot, mattered not,
     It went down him like a shot, but he still stood the test.

3.   He swallowed tripe and lard by the yard, we got scared,
     We thought it would go hard when the waiter brought the bill
     We told him to give o'er, but he swore he could lower
     Twice as much again and more before he had his fill.
     He nearly supped a trough full of broth says McGrath,
     "He'll devour the tablecloth if you don't hold him in."
     When the waiter brought the charge, McEldoo felt so large
     He began to scowl and barge and his blood went on fire.

4.   He began to curse and swear tear his hair in despair
     And to finish the affair called the shopman a liar.
     The shopman he drew out, and no doubt, he did clout
     McEldoo he kicked about like an old football
     He tattered all his clothes, broke his nose, I suppose
     He'd have killed him with a few blows in no time at all.

5.   McEldoo began to howl and to growl, by my sowl
     He threw an empty bowl at the shopkeepers head.
     It struck poor Mickey Flynn, peeled the skin off his chin
     And the ructions did begin and we all fought and bled.
     The peelers did arrive, man alive, four or five,
     At us they made a drive for us all to march away.
     We paid for all the mate, that we ate, stood a trate,
     And went home to reminate on the spree that day.

I'LL TELL MY MA

Every town in Ireland has its own version of this children's street song.

Lively

I'll tell my ma when I go home The boys won't leave the girls a-lone. They pulled my hair and stole my comb, But that's all right till I go home. She is hand-some She is pret-ty, She is the belle of Bel-fast cit-y; She is court-in' one, two, three, Please, won't you tell me who is he?

All the boys are fighting for her,
They rap at the door and they ring at the bell
Sayin', "O my true love are you well?"
Out she comes as white as snow,
Rings on her fingers and bells on her toes
Ould Johnny Murray says she'll die
If she doesn't get the fellow with the roving eye.

Let the wind and the rain and the hail blow high,
And the snow come travelling from the sky,
She's as nice as apple pie,
And she'll get her own lad by and by.
When she gets a lad of her own
She won't tell her ma when she comes home
Let them all come as they will,
For it's Albert Mooney she loves still.

THE WILD COLONIAL BOY

Arranged and Adapted by TOM CLANCY, LIAM CLANCY, PAT CLANCY, TOMMY MAKEM. © Copyright 1962, 1963 by TIPARM
Music Publishers, Inc. International Copyright Secured. All Rights Reserved. Printed in U.S.A.

Any man who could defy the law as gallantly as Jack Duggan had to become a hero (the law being British).

Brightly

1. There was a wild co - lon - ial boy, Jack Dug - gan was his name. He was born and raised in Ire - land, In a place called Cas - tle - maine. He was his fa - ther's on - ly son, his moth - er's pride and joy And dear - ly did his par - ents love The Wild Co - lon - ial Boy.

2. At the early age of sixteen years he left his native home,
And to Australia's sunny shore he was inclined to roam.
He robbed the rich, he helped the poor, he shot James McAvoy
A terror to Australia was The Wild Colonial Boy.

3. One morning on the prairie as Jack he rode along.
A-listening to the mocking bird a-singing a cheerful song
Out stepped a band of troopers, Kelly Davis and Fitzroy
They all set out to capture him, The Wild Colonial Boy.

4. "Surrender now, Jack Duggan, for you see we're three to one
Surrender in the Queen's high name for you're a plundering son."
Jack drew two pistols from his belt and proudly waved them high
"I'll fight, but not surrender," said The Wild Colonial Boy.

5. He fired a shot at Kelly which brought him to the ground
And turning 'round to Davis he received a fatal wound
A bullet pierced his proud young heart from the pistol of Fitzroy
And that was how they captured him, The Wild Colonial Boy.

MY JOHNNY LAD

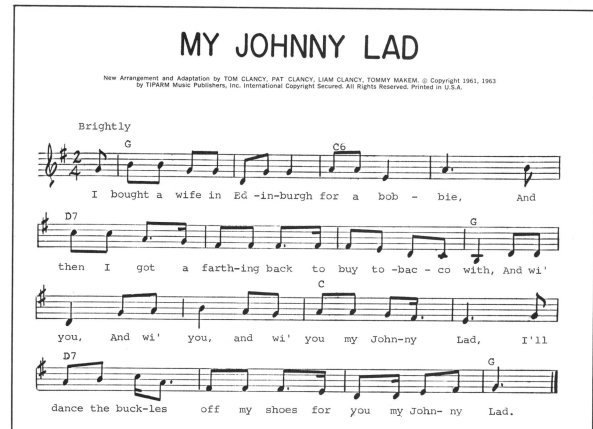

Brightly

I bought a wife in Ed-in-burgh for a bob-bie, And then I got a farth-ing back to buy to-bac-co with, And wi' you, And wi' you, and wi' you my John-ny Lad, I'll dance the buck-les off my shoes for you my John-ny Lad.

2. As I was walkin' Sunday, 'twas there I saw the Queen,
   A-playin' at the football with the lads on Glasgow green
   And wi' you, and wi' you, and wi' you my Johnny lad,
   I'll dance the buckles off my shoes for you my Johnny lad.

3. The captain 'o the other side was scorin' with great style,
   The queen, she called a policeman, and had him thrown in jail,
   And wi' you, and wi' you, and wi' you my Johnny lad,
   I'll dance the buckles off my shoes for you my Johnny lad.

4. Samson was a mighty man, and he fought with the cuddy's jaw,
   He fought a thousand battles wearing crimson flannel drawers,
   And wi' you, and wi' you, and wi' you my Johnny lad,
   I'll dance the buckless off my shoes for you my Johnny lad.

5. Napoleon was an emperor, and he ruled on land and sea,
   He ruled all France and Germany, but he didn't rule Jock McGee
   And wi' you, and wi' you, and wi' you my Johnny lad,
   I'll dance the buckles off my shoes for you my Johnny lad.

6. Now Johnny is a bonny lad, he is a lad of mine,
   I've never had a better lad and I've had twenty-nine,
   And wi' you, and wi' you, and wi' you my Johnny lad,
   I'll dance the buckles off my shoes for you my Johnny lad.

YOUNG RODDY M'CORLEY

Arranged and Adapted by PAT CLANCY. © Copyright 1961, 1963 by TIPARM Music Publishers, Inc. International Copyright
Secured. All Rights Reserved. Printed in U.S.A.

Roddy McCorley was hanged for his part in Toomebridge, County
Antrim, 1798 Rising.

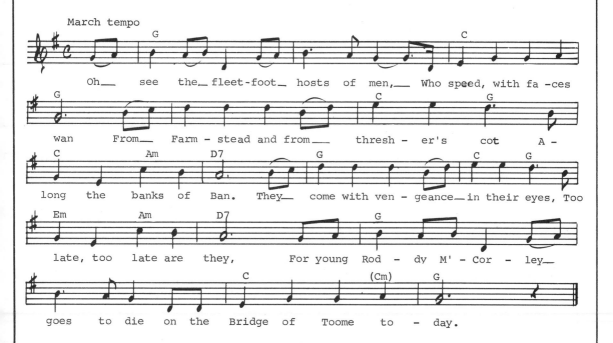

March tempo

Oh__ see the__ fleet-foot__ hosts of men,__ Who speed, with fa -ces
wan From__ Farm - stead and from__ thresh - er's cot A -
long the banks of Ban. They__ come with ven - geance__ in their eyes, Too
late, too late are they, For young Rod - dy M' - Cor - ley__
goes to die on the Bridge of Toome to - day.

Up the narrow street he stepped,
Smiling and proud and young;
About the hemp-robe on his neck
The golden ringlets clung.
There's never a tear in his blue eyes,
Both glad and bright are they
As Young Roddy M'Corley goes to die
On the Bridge of Toome today.

When he last stepped up that street
His shining pike in hand,
Behind him marched in grim array
A stalwart earnest band!
For Antrim Town! for Antrim Town!
He led them to the fray
As Young Roddy M'Corley goes to die
On the Bridge of Toome today.

There's never a one of all your dead
More bravely fell in fray,
Than he who marches to his fate
On the Bridge of Toome today.
True to the last, true to the last,
He treads the upward way
And Young Roddy M'Corley goes to die
On the Bridge of Toome today.

WHEN I WAS SINGLE

Arranged and Adapted by PAT CLANCY, TOM CLANCY, LIAM CLANCY, TOMMY MAKEM, DAVID HAMMOND. © Copyright 1962,
1963 by TIPARM Music Publishers, Inc. International Copyright Secured. All Rights Reserved. Printed in U.S.A.

This song tells why people in Ireland tend not to marry.

Moderately bright

1. When I was single, I wore a plaid shawl, Now that I'm married I've nothing at all. Oh but still I

(Chorus) love him, I'll for-give him, I'll go with him where-ev-er he goes.

2. He came up our alley and he whistled me out,
   But the tail of his shirt, from the trousers hung out.

   (Chorus)

3. He bought me a handkerchief, red, white and blue,
   But before I could wear it, he tore it in two.

   (Chorus)

4. He brought me to an ale house, and he bought me some stout,
   But before I could drink it he, ordered me out.

   (Chorus)

5. He borrowed some money to buy me a ring,
   Then he and the jeweler went off on a fling.

   (Chorus)

6. There's cakes in the oven, there's cheese on the shelf,
   If you want any more, you can sing it yourself.

   (Chorus)

WILL YE GO, LASSIE, GO?

Arranged and adapted by David Hammond, Liam Clancy, Pat Clancy, Tom Clancy & Tommy Makem. Copyright
©1962 by Tiparm Music Publishers Inc. All Rights Reserved. International Copyright Secured. Printed in U.S.A.

By process of time, this song was distilled from an old written Scottish
ballad called "The Beaes of Balguitter."

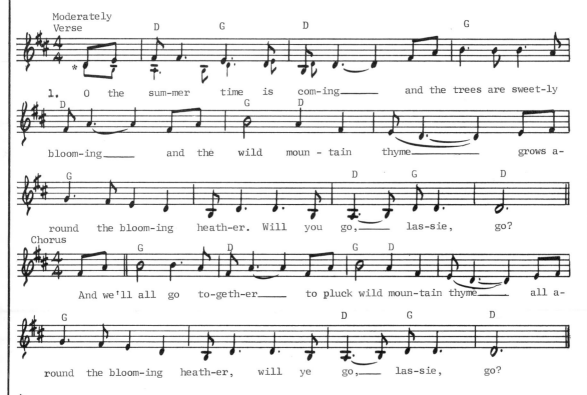

1. O the summer time is coming and the trees are sweetly
blooming and the wild moun-tain thyme grows a-
round the blooming heather. Will you go, las-sie, go?

Chorus
And we'll all go to-geth-er to pluck wild moun-tain thyme all a-
round the blooming heather, will ye go, las-sie, go?

*Small notes variants for 2nd and 3rd verses

2. I will build my love a tower
    Near yon pure crystal fountain
    And on it I will pile
    All the flowers of the mountain
    Will ye go, lassie, go?

    (Chorus)

3. If my true love, she were gone
    I would surely find another
    Where wild mountain thyme
    Grows around the blooming heather
    Will ye go, lassie, go?

    (Chorus)

    Repeat Verse 1

OLD WOMAN FROM WEXFORD

By SEAMUS ENNIS, Dublin; Arranged by PAT CLANCY. © Copyright 1962, 1963 by TIPARM Music Publishers, Inc. International
Copyright Secured. All Rights Reserved. Printed in U.S.A.

If you want to get rid of your husband, don't try it this way.

VERSE

Moderately

There was an ould wo-man in Wex-ford, In Wex - ford Town did dwell,— She loved her hus-band dear - ly, But an - oth - er man twice as well.

CHORUS

With me right fol lid-der-al ar - yl, And me right fol low-rel ee.—

2. One day she went to the doctor
Some medicine for to find
Saying, "Doctor, give me something
That'll make me ould man blind." (Chorus)

3. O, feed him eggs and marrow bones
And make him sup them all
And it won't be so very long after
That'll he won't see you at all. (Chorus)

4. So she fed him eggs and marrow bones
And made him sup them all
And it wasn't so very long after
That'll he couldn't see the wall. (Chorus)

5. "O," says he, "I'd go and drown meself,
But that might be a sin."
"Well," says she, "I'll go along with you
And I'll help to push you in." (Chorus)

6. The old woman, she went back a bit
To get a running go,
The old man blithely stepped aside
And she went in below. (Chorus)

7. O, how loudly did she roar,
And how loudly did she bawl,
"Arra hould you whist ould women," says he.
"Sure I can't see you at all." (Chorus)

8. She swam and swam and swam and swam
Till she came to the further brim
The old man got a long larch pole
And he pushed her further in. (Chorus)

9. O, eggs are eggs and marrow bones
   Will make your old man blind,
   But if you want to drown him
   You must creep up close behind.

A BIG SHIP SAILING

Arranged and Adapted by JOAN CLANCY, PAT CLANCY, TOM CLANCY, LIAM CLANCY, TOMMY MAKEM. © Copyright 1963 by TIPARM Music Publishers, Inc. International Copyright Secured. All Rights Reserved. Printed in U.S.A.

The "illy-ally-P" was our childhood word for the sea. From Mrs. Joan Clancy.

Lively

There's a big ship sail - - ing on the il - li - al - lay oh, The il - li - ay - lay oh, The il - li - al - lay oh. There's a big ship sail - ing on the il - li - al - lay oh, Heigh - ho, il - li - al - lay oh.

2. There's a big ship sailing, rocking on the sea,
        rocking on the sea, rocking on the sea.
    There's a big ship sailing, rocking on the sea.
    Heigh-ho, rocking on the sea.

3. There's a big ship sailing back again.
        back again, back again.
    There's a big ship sailing back again,
    Heigh-ho, back again.

BALLINDERRY

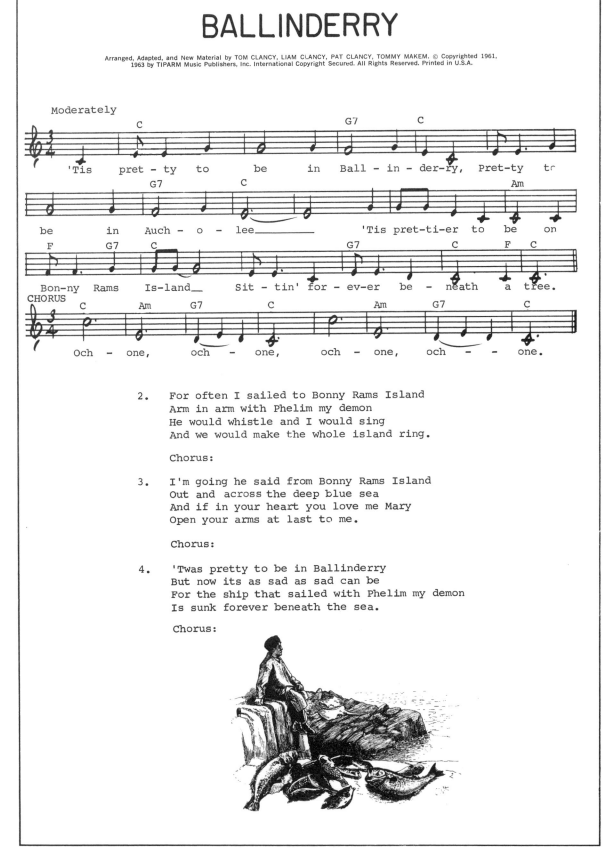

Moderately

'Tis pret - ty to be in Ball - in - der-ry, Pret-ty to be in Auch - o - lee____ 'Tis pret-ti-er to be on Bon-ny Rams Is-land__ Sit - tin' for - ev-er be - neath a tree.

CHORUS

Och - one, och - one, och - one, och - - one.

2. For often I sailed to Bonny Rams Island
   Arm in arm with Phelim my demon
   He would whistle and I would sing
   And we would make the whole island ring.

   Chorus:

3. I'm going he said from Bonny Rams Island
   Out and across the deep blue sea
   And if in your heart you love me Mary
   Open your arms at last to me.

   Chorus:

4. 'Twas pretty to be in Ballinderry
   But now its as sad as sad can be
   For the ship that sailed with Phelim my demon
   Is sunk forever beneath the sea.

   Chorus:

JOHNSON'S MOTOR CAR

Arranged and Adapted by LIAM CLANCY. © Copyright 1963 by TIPARM Music Publishers, Inc. International Copyright Secured. All Rights Reserved. Printed in U.S.A.

During the war of Independence, the I.R.A. had very little compunction about commandeering someone's car for their own uses. Especially if it happened to belong to an old Protestant doctor who was rather unpopular.

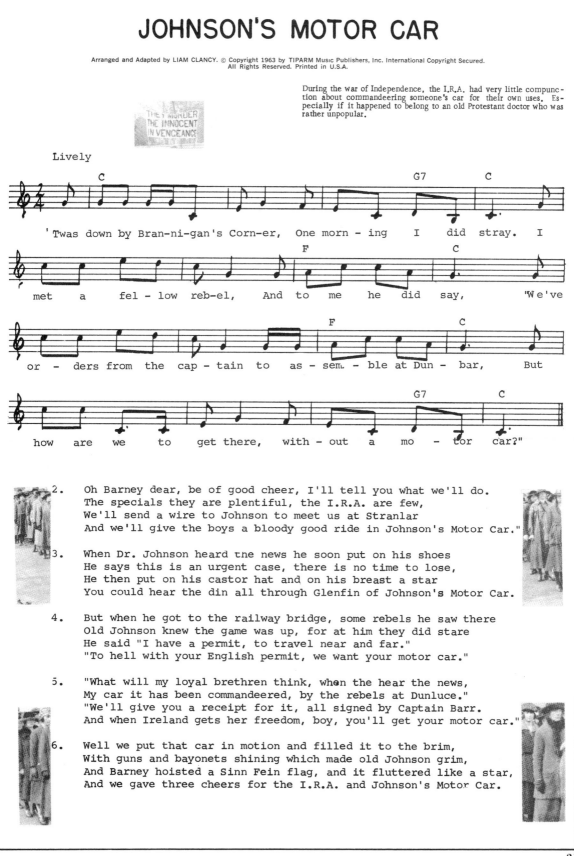

Lively

'Twas down by Bran-ni-gan's Corn-er, One morn-ing I did stray. I met a fel-low reb-el, And to me he did say, "We've or-ders from the cap-tain to as-sem-ble at Dun-bar, But how are we to get there, with-out a mo-tor car?"

2. Oh Barney dear, be of good cheer, I'll tell you what we'll do.
The specials they are plentiful, the I.R.A. are few,
We'll send a wire to Johnson to meet us at Stranlar
And we'll give the boys a bloody good ride in Johnson's Motor Car."

3. When Dr. Johnson heard the news he soon put on his shoes
He says this is an urgent case, there is no time to lose,
He then put on his castor hat and on his breast a star
You could hear the din all through Glenfin of Johnson's Motor Car.

4. But when he got to the railway bridge, some rebels he saw there
Old Johnson knew the game was up, for at him they did stare
He said "I have a permit, to travel near and far."
"To hell with your English permit, we want your motor car."

5. "What will my loyal brethren think, when the hear the news,
My car it has been commandeered, by the rebels at Dunluce."
"We'll give you a receipt for it, all signed by Captain Barr.
And when Ireland gets her freedom, boy, you'll get your motor car."

6. Well we put that car in motion and filled it to the brim,
With guns and bayonets shining which made old Johnson grim,
And Barney hoisted a Sinn Fein flag, and it fluttered like a star,
And we gave three cheers for the I.R.A. and Johnson's Motor Car.

COURTIN' IN THE KITCHEN

Lively tempo

Come sin-gle belle and beau, Un-to me pay at-ten-tion. Don't ever fall in love, It's the dev-il's own in-ven-tion. Once I fell in love with a maid-en so be-witch-in' Miss Hen-ri-et-ta Bell out of Captain Kelly's kitchen. With my too-ral-oo-ral-I and my too-ral-oo-ral-ad-dy With my too-ral-oo-ral-I and my too-ral-oo-ral-ad-dy.

2. At the age of seventeen, I was 'prenticed to a grocer
    Not far from Stephen's Green, where Miss Henry used to go sir
    Her manners were sublime and she set my heart a-twitchin'
    And she invited me to a hooley in the kitchen.
    (Chorus)

3. Next Sunday being the day that we were to have the "flare up,"
    I dressed myself quite gay, and I frizzed and oiled my hair up
    The captain had no wife, faith he had gone out fishin'
    And we kicked up high life, down below stairs in the kitchen.
    (Chorus)

4. With her arms around my waist, she slyly hinted marriage,
    To the door in dreadful haste, came Captain Kelly's carriage
    Her eyes soon filled with hate and poison she was spittin'
    When the captain at the door walked right into the kitchen.
    (Chorus)

5. When the captain came downstairs though he saw my situation,
    In spite of all my prayers, I was marched off to the station
    For me they'd take no bail, but to get home I was itchin'
    And I had to tell the tale, how I came into the kitchen.
    (Chorus)

6. I said she did invite me, but she gave a flat denial
    For assault she did indict me, and I was sent for trial
    She swore I robbed the house, in spite of all her screechin'
    And I got six months "hard" for my Courtin' In The Kitchen.
    (Chorus)

SOUTH AUSTRALIA

A lively, optimistic sailors' song.

With vigor

In South Aus-tra-lia I was born, Heave a - way, Haul a - way, In
South Aus - tra-lia 'round Cape Horn, We're bound for South Aus-tra-lia.

CHORUS

Haul a - way, your roll-ing King, Heave a - way, Haul a - way,
Haul a - way, Oh hear me sing, We're bound for South Aus - tra-lia.

2. As I walked out one morning fair,
   Heave away, haul away,
   'Twas there I met Miss Nancy Blair,
   We're bound for South Australia.
   (Chorus)

3. I shook her up, I shook her down,
   Heave away, haul away,
   I shook her round and round the town,
   We're bound for South Australia.
   (Chorus)

4. There ain't but one thing grieves my mind,
   Heave away, haul away,
   To leave Miss Nancy Blair behind,
   We're bound for South Australia.
   (Chorus)

5. And as we wallop around Cape Horn,
   Heave away, haul away,
   You'll wish to God you'd never been born,
   We're bound for South Australia.
   (Chorus)

ROSIN THE BOW

Arranged and Adapted by PAT CLANCY. © Copyright 1961, 1963 by TIPARM Music Publishers, Inc. International Copyright Secured. All Rights Reserved. Printed in U.S.A.

This old fiddle-player must have led a great life; even at the edge of the grave, he could sing a song about it.

Moderately bright

I've trav - elled all o - ver this world _____ And now to an - oth - er I go _____ And I know that good quar - ters are wait - ing _____ To wel - come Old Ros - in the Bow. _____

CHORUS

To wel - come Old Ros - in the Bow, _____ To wel - come Old Ros - in the Bow, _____ And I know that good quar - ters are wait - ing _____ To wel - come Old Ros - in the Bow.

2. When I'm dead and laid out on the counter
   A voice you will hear from below
   Saying send down a hogshead of whisky
   To drink with old rosin the bow.

Chorus: To drink with old rosin the bow
           To drink with old rosin the bow
           Saying send down a hogshead of whisky
           To drink with old rosin the bow.

3. And get a half dozen stout fellows
   And stack em all up in a row
   Let them drink out of half gallon bottles
   To the memory of rosin the bow.

Chorus: To the memory of Rosin The Bow
           To the memory of Rosin The Bow
           Let them drink out of half gallon bottles
           To the memory of Rosin The Bow

24

4. Get this half dozen stout fellows
    And let them all stagger and go
    And dig a great hole in the meadow
    And in it put Rosin The Bow.

Chorus: And in it put Rosin The Bow
           And in it put Rosin The Bow
           And dig a great hole in the meadow
           And in it put Rosin The Bow.

5. Get ye a couple of bottles
    Put one at me head and me toe
    With a diamond ring scratch upon them
    The name of old Rosin The Bow.

Chorus: The name of old Rosin The Bow
           The name of old Rosin The Bow
           With a diamond ring scratch upon them
           The name of old Rosin The Bow.

6. I feel that old tyrant approaching
    That cruel remorseless old foe
    And I lift up me glass in his honor
    Take a drink with Old Rosin The Bow.

Chorus: Take a drink with old Rosin The Bow
           Take a drink with old Rosin The Bow
           And I lift up me glass in his honor
           Take a drink with old Rosin The Bow.

KELLY THE BOY FROM KILLANE

Arranged and Adapted by TOM CLANCY. © Copyright 1963 by TIPARM Music Publishers, Inc. International Copyright Secured.
All Rights Reserved. Printed in U.S.A.

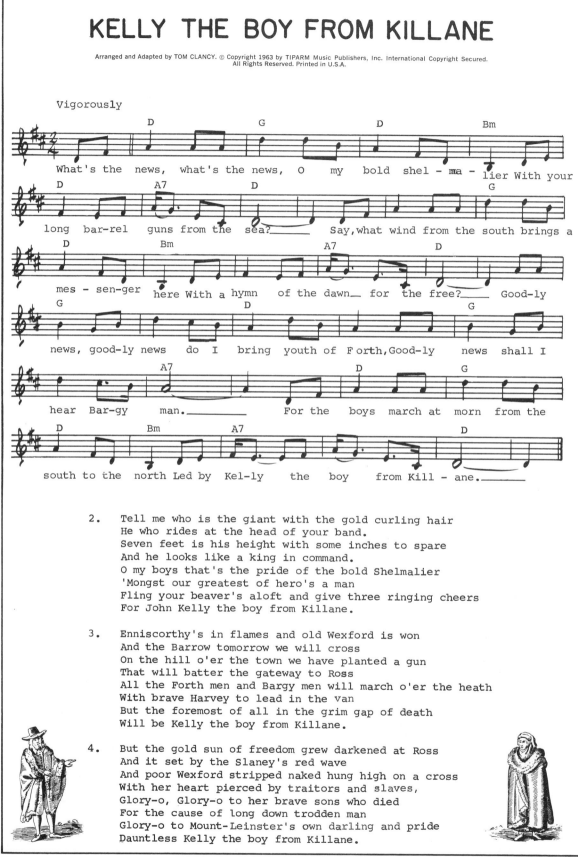

Vigorously

What's the news, what's the news, O my bold shel - ma - lier With your
long bar-rel guns from the sea? Say, what wind from the south brings a
mes - sen-ger here With a hymn of the dawn for the free? Good-ly
news, good-ly news do I bring youth of Forth, Good-ly news shall I
hear Bar-gy man. For the boys march at morn from the
south to the north Led by Kel-ly the boy from Kill - ane.

2. Tell me who is the giant with the gold curling hair
   He who rides at the head of your band.
   Seven feet is his height with some inches to spare
   And he looks like a king in command.
   O my boys that's the pride of the bold Shelmalier
   'Mongst our greatest of hero's a man
   Fling your beaver's aloft and give three ringing cheers
   For John Kelly the boy from Killane.

3. Enniscorthy's in flames and old Wexford is won
   And the Barrow tomorrow we will cross
   On the hill o'er the town we have planted a gun
   That will batter the gateway to Ross
   All the Forth men and Bargy men will march o'er the heath
   With brave Harvey to lead in the van
   But the foremost of all in the grim gap of death
   Will be Kelly the boy from Killane.

4. But the gold sun of freedom grew darkened at Ross
   And it set by the Slaney's red wave
   And poor Wexford stripped naked hung high on a cross
   With her heart pierced by traitors and slaves,
   Glory-o, Glory-o to her brave sons who died
   For the cause of long down trodden man
   Glory-o to Mount-Leinster's own darling and pride
   Dauntless Kelly the boy from Killane.

THE MOONSHINER

Spritely

I've been a moon-shin-er for man-y a year, I've spent all my mon-ey on whis-key and beer, I'll go to some hol-low and I'll set up my still, And I'll make you a gal-lon for a ten shill-ing bill.

CHORUS

I'm a ram-bler, I'm a gam-bler, I'm a long ways from home, And if you don't like me, Well leave me a-lone. I'll eat when I'm hun-gry And I'll drink when I'm dry, And if moon-shine don't kill me, I'll live till I die.

2. I'll go to some hollow in this country,
    Ten gallons of wash, I can go on a spree,
    No woman to follow, the world is all mine,
    And I love none so well as I love the moonshine.

        Chorus:

3. O moonshine, dear moonshine, o how I love thee
    You killed me old father but dare you kill me,
    O bless all moonshiners and bless all moonshine
    Oh its breath smells as sweet as the dew on the
        vine.

        Chorus:

27

MOUNTAIN DEW

Arranged and Adapted by PAT CLANCY, TOM CLANCY, LIAM CLANCY, TOMMY MAKEM. © Copyright 1962, 1963 by TIPARM
Music Publishers, Inc. International Copyright Secured. All Rights Reserved. Printed in U.S.A.

"Mountain dew" is illegal homemade whiskey.

Moderately bright

1. Let grass-es grow and wat-ers flow in a free and ea-sy way, but give me e-nough of the fine old stuff that's made near Gal-way Bay, And po-lice-men all__ from Do-ne-gal,__ Sli-go and Leit-rim, too, we'll give them the slip and we'll take a sip of the real old moun-tain dew.

Chorus

Hi-the did-dle-y - I-dill-um, did-dle-y-doo-dle-I-dill-um did-dle-y-doo - ri - did-dle-y-di - day, Hi-the did-dle-y - I-dill - um, did-dle-y-doo-dill-I- dill-um, did-dle - y - doo - ri, did-dle - y - di - day.

At the foot of the hill there's a neat little still, where the
    smoke curls up to the sky
By the smoke and the smell, you can plainly tell that there's
    poteen brewing near by,
For it fills the air, with odor rare, and betwixt both me and you,
When home you stroll, you can take a bowl, or a bucket of the
    mountain dew.

(Chorus)

Now learned men who use the pen, have wrote your praises high,
That sweet poteen from Ireland green, distilled from wheat and rye
Throw away your pills, it will cure all ills, of pagan Christian
    or Jew,
Take off your coat and grease your throat, with the real old
    mountain dew.

(Chorus)

28

MR. MOSES RI-TOORAL-I-AY

Arranged and Adapted by PAT CLANCY, LIAM CLANCY, TOM CLANCY, TOMMY MAKEM. © Copyright 1962, 1963 by TIPARM Music Publishers, Inc. International Copyright Secured. All Rights Reserved. Printed in U.S.A.

Brightly

The po - lice - man walked out Oh so proud on his beat, When a vi - sion came to him of stripes on his sleeve. "Pro - mo - tion", He whis - pered, "I'll try for to - day. So come with me Mis - ter Ri - too - ral - i - ay.

2. "Come tell me your name" says the limb of the law,
To the little fat man selling wares on the straw,
"What's that Sir? Me name sir? Why 'tis there on display,
And it's Moses Ri-tooral-I-ooral-I-ay."

3. Now the trial it came on and it lasted a week.
One judge said 'twas German, another 'twas Greek.
"Prove you're Irish" said the policeman "and beyond it say nay,
And we'll sit on it Moses Ri-tooral-I-ay."

4. Now the prisoner stepped up there as stiff as a crutch.
"Are you Irish or English or German or Dutch?"
"I'm a Jew sir, I'm a Jew sir that came over to stay
And my name it is Moses Ri-tooral-I-ay."

5. "We're two of a kind" said the judge to the Jew.
You're a cousin of Briscoe and I am one too.
This numbskull has blundered and for it will pay"
"Wisha that's right" says Moses.Ri-tooral-I-ay.

6. There's a garbage collector who works down our street,
He once was a policeman, the pride of his beat,
And he moans all the night and he groans all the day,
Singing Moses Ri-tooral-I-ooral-I-ay.

THE OLD ORANGE FLUTE

New Arrangement and Adaptation by TOMMY MAKEM. © Copyright 1961, 1963 by TIPARM Music Publishers, Inc. International Copyright Secured. All Rights Reserved. Printed in U.S.A.

Moderately

1. In the Coun-ty Ty-rone near the town of Dun-gan-non, where man-y the ruc-tions me-self had a han' in, Bob Wil-liam-son lived, a wea-ver by trade, and all of us thought him a stout Or-ange blade. On the twelfth of Ju-ly as it year-ly did come, Bob played with his flute to the sound of a drum. You may talk of your harp, your pi-an-o, or lute, but there's none can com-pare with the old or-ange flute.

2. Now Bob the deceiver, he took us all in,
   He married a Papist named Bridget McGinn,
   Turned Papish himself, and forsook the old cause,
   That gave us our freedom, religion and laws.
   Now the boys of the place made some comment upon it.
   And Bob had to fly to the province of Connaught,
   He fled with his wife and his fixings to boot,
   And along with the latter his old Orange flute.

3. At the chapel on Sunday to atone for past deeds,
   Said paters and aves and counted his beads,
   'Til after some time at the priest's own desire,
   He went with the old flute to play in the choir.
   He went with the old flute for to play for the mass,
   But the instrument shivered, and sighed, oh, alas,
   And try though he would, though it made a great noise,
   The flute would play only "The Protestant Boys."

4. Bob jumped and he started and got in a flutter,
   And threw the old flute in the blessed holy water,
   He thought that this charm would bring some other sound,
   When he tried it again it played "Croppies Lie Down."
   Now for all he could whistle and finger and blow,
   To play Papish music he found it no go,
   "Kick the Pope," and "Boil Water" it freely would sound,
   But one Papish squeak in it couldn't be found.

5. At the council of priests that was held the next day,
   They decided to banish the old flute away,
   They couldn't knock heresy out of its head,
   So they bought Bob a new one to play in its stead.
   Now the old flute was doomed, and its fate was pathetic
   'Twas fastened and burned at the stake as heretic,
   As the flames soared around it, they heard a strange noise,
   'Twas the old flute still whistling "The Protestant Boys."
   Toora lu, toora lay, oh it's six miles from Bangor to Donnahadee.

PORTLAIRGE

Arranged and Adapted by PAT CLANCY, TOM CLANCY, LIAM CLANCY, TOMMY MAKEM, JACK KEENAN. © Copyright 1961, 1963 by TIPARM Music Publishers, Inc. International Copyright Secured. All Rights Reserved. Printed in U.S.A.

Brightly

O the vlos- a law ih Bort Lawr-iga Fol dow fol dee fol the dad I liom Vee feen iss pwints er clawr oun Fol dow fol dee fol the dad I liom. Vee lawn a tee the vnawv oun. Fol dow fol dee fol the dad I liom. Og us mish -a eg eel slainte Fol dow fol dee fol the dad I liom.

2. Au ge steghey bor auh raurren
Fol dow fol dee fol the dad I lum
Au gus trur oh tibber u dawh
Fol dow fol dee fol the dad I lum
Near rev a weenter sauss
Fol dow fol dee fol the dad I lum
Near rauther auch la hosta
Fol dow fol dee fol the dad I lum.

3. Auh riotsa oun correg amorouk
Fol dow fol dee fol the dad I lum
Au gus taira colleen brahlum
Fol dow fol dee fol the dad I lum
Yo mead tree dum maurnin
Fol dow fol dee fol the dad I lum
Oh brog cor tibera dor
Fol dow fol dee fol the dad I lum

TIM FINNEGAN'S WAKE

But the war was over when the liquor scattered over Tim.

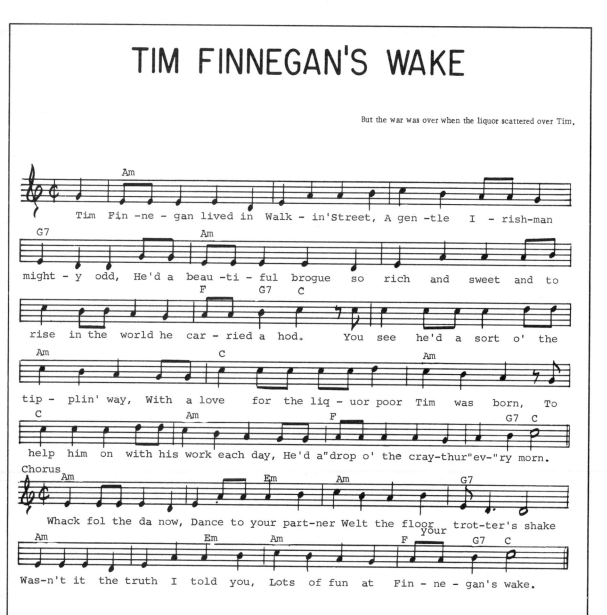

Tim Fin-ne-gan lived in Walk-in'Street, A gen-tle I-rish-man might-y odd, He'd a beau-ti-ful brogue so rich and sweet and to rise in the world he car-ried a hod. You see he'd a sort o' the tip-plin' way, With a love for the liq-uor poor Tim was born, To help him on with his work each day, He'd a"drop o' the cray-thur"ev-"ry morn.

Chorus

Whack fol the da now, Dance to your part-ner Welt the floor your trot-ter's shake Was-n't it the truth I told you, Lots of fun at Fin-ne-gan's wake.

One mornin' Tim was rather full,
His head felt heavy which made him shake,
He fell from a ladder, and he broke his skull,
And they carried him home his corpse to wake.
They rolled him up in a nice clean sheet
And laid him out upon the bed,
With a gallon of whisky at his feet,
And a barrel of porter at his head.

     - Chorus -

His friends assembled at the wake,
And Mrs. Finnegan called for lunch,
First they brought in tay, and cake,
Then pipes, tobacco and whisky punch.
Biddy O'Brien began to cry,
Such a nice clean corpse did you ever see?
Tim Mavourneen why did you die?
Arrah hold your gob said Paddy McGhee.

     - Chorus -

Then Maggie O'Connor took up the job,
Oh Biddy says she, you're wrong I'm sure
Biddy gave her a belt in the gob,
And left her sprawling on the floor.
Then the war did soon engage,
'Twas woman to woman, and man to man,
Shelelaigh law was all the rage,
And a row, and a ruction soon began.

     - Chorus -

Then Mickey Maloney raised his head,
When a noggin of whisky flew at him,
It missed and falling on the bed,
The liquor scattered over Tim.
Tim revives see how he rises,
Timothy rising from the bed,
Said, "Whirl your whisky around like
        blazes,
Thanum an dial do you think I'm dead?"
     - Chorus -

BOLD O'DONAHUE

Moderately

Well here I am from Pad-dy's land, a land of high re-nown, I broke the hearts of all the girls for miles 'round Kea-dy Town. And when they hear that I'm a-wa they'll raise a hul-la-ba-loo, When they hear a-bout that hand-some lad that they call O' Don - a - hue.

Refrain

For I'm the boy to please her and I'm the boy to tease her, I'm the boy can squeeze her ach and I'll tell you what I'll do. "I'll court her like an I-rish-man And the brogue and blar-ney too is my plan, With the rol-li-gan, swol-li-gan, hol-li - gan, wol-li - gan, Bold O' Don - a - hue.

I wish my love was a red, red rose growing on yon garden wall,
And me to be a dewdrop and upon her brow I'd fall,
Perhaps now she might think on me as a rather heavy dew,
And no more she'd love that handsome lad that they call O'Donahue

(Chorus)

Well I hear that Queen Victoria has a daughter fine and grand,
Perhaps she'd take it into her head for to marry an Irishman,
And if I could only get the chance to have a word or two,
I'm sure she'd take a notion in the Bold O'Donahue.

(Chorus)

A MAN OF DOUBLE DEED

Arranged and Adapted by JOAN CLANCY, PAT CLANCY, TOM CLANCY, LIAM CLANCY, TOMMY MAKEM. © Copyright 1963 by
TIPARM Music Publishers, Inc. International Copyright Secured. All Rights Reserved. Printed in U.S.A.

A beautiful mystic poem created by children to frighten themselves.

HAUL AWAY JOE

New Arrangement and Adaptation by TOM CLANCY, PAT CLANCY, LIAM CLANCY, TOMMY MAKEM. © Copyright 1961, 1963 by TIPARM Music Publishers, Inc. International Copyright Secured. All Rights Reserved. Printed in U.S.A.

Slowly

1. When I was a lit-tle boy____ so my moth - er told me, to me, way haul a - way, we'll haul a - way Joe.

2. That if I did not kiss the girls, my lips would all grow mouldy, to me,
   Way, haul away, we'll haul away Joe.

3. Way, haul away, the good ship now is rolling, to me,
   Way, haul away, we'll haul away Joe.

4. First I met a Yankee girl and she was fat and lazy, to me,
   Way, haul away, we'll haul away Joe.

5. Then I met an Irish girl, she damn near drove me crazy, to me,
   Way, haul away, we'll haul away Joe.

6. King Louis was the king of France before the revolution,
   Way, haul away, we'll haul away Joe.

7. And then he got his head cut off, it spoiled his constitution,
   Way, haul away, we'll haul away Joe.

8. Way, haul away, we're bound for better weather, to me,
   Way, haul away, we'll haul away Joe.

REILLY'S DAUGHTER

New Arrangement and Adaptation by TOM CLANCY, PAT CLANCY, LIAM CLANCY, TOMMY MAKEM. © Copyright 1961, 1963
by TIPARM Music Publishers, Inc. International Copyright Secured. All Rights Reserved. Printed in U.S.A.

A vaudeville song that has many versions, not all printable.

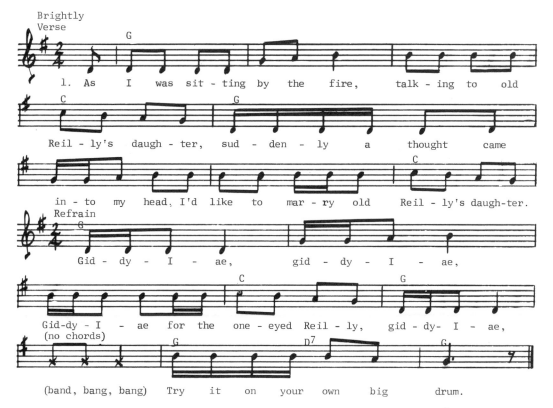

Brightly
Verse

1. As I was sit-ting by the fire, talk-ing to old Reil-ly's daugh-ter, sud-den-ly a thought came in-to my head. I'd like to mar-ry old Reil-ly's daugh-ter.

Refrain

Gid-dy-I-ae, gid-dy-I-ae, Gid-dy-I-ae for the one-eyed Reil-ly, gid-dy-I-ae, (no chords) (band, bang, bang) Try it on your own big drum.

2. Reilly played on the big bass drum,
Reilly had a mind for murder and slaughter,
Reilly had a bright red, glittering eye,
And he kept that eye on his lovely daughter.

3. Her hair was black and her eyes were blue,
The colonel, and the major and the captain sought her,
The sergeant, and the private and the drummer boy, too,
But they never had a chance with Reilly's daughter.

4. I got me a ring and a parson, too,
Got me a scratch in a married quarter,
Settled me down to a peaceful life,
Happy as a king with Reilly's daughter.

5. Suddenly a footstep on the stairs,
Who should it be but Reilly out for slaughter,
With two pistols in his hands,
Looking for the man who had married his daughter.

6. I caught old Reilly by the hair,
Rammed his head in a pail of water,
Fired his pistols into the air,
A damned sight quicker than I married his daughter.

THE BARNYARDS OF DELGATY

Arranged and Adapted by PAT CLANCY, TOM CLANCY, LIAM CLANCY, TOMMY MAKEM. © Copyright 1962, 1963 by TIPARM
Music Publishers, Inc. International Copyright Secured. All Rights Reserved. Printed in U.S.A.

One of the body of Scottish songs belonging to the farm laborers;
called the Bothy Ballads. They were mostly rather risque.

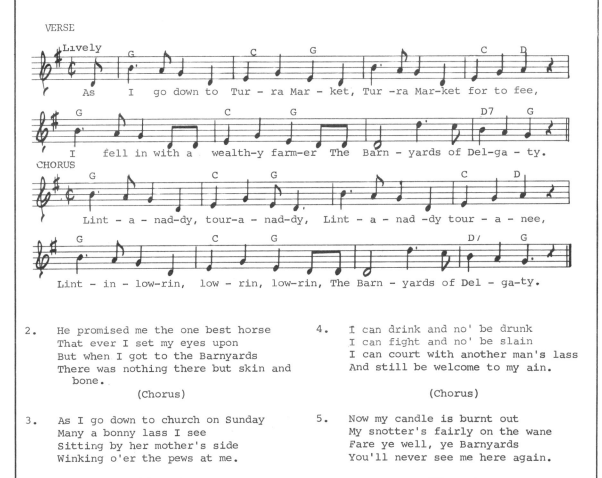

VERSE

As I go down to Tur - ra Mar - ket, Tur -ra Mar-ket for to fee,
I fell in with a wealth-y farm-er The Barn - yards of Del-ga - ty.

CHORUS

Lint - a - nad-dy, tour-a - nad-dy, Lint - a - nad -dy tour - a - nee,
Lint - in - low-rin, low - rin, low-rin, The Barn - yards of Del - ga-ty.

2. He promised me the one best horse
That ever I set my eyes upon
But when I got to the Barnyards
There was nothing there but skin and
   bone.
         (Chorus)

3. As I go down to church on Sunday
Many a bonny lass I see
Sitting by her mother's side
Winking o'er the pews at me.

         (Chorus)

4. I can drink and no' be drunk
I can fight and no' be slain
I can court with another man's lass
And still be welcome to my ain.

         (Chorus)

5. Now my candle is burnt out
My snotter's fairly on the wane
Fare ye well, ye Barnyards
You'll never see me here again.

         (Chorus)

IRISH ROVER

Arranged and Adapted by PAT CLANCY, LIAM CLANCY, TOM CLANCY, TOMMY MAKEM. © Copyright 1962, 1963 by TIPARM
Music Publishers, Inc. International Copyright Secured. All Rights Reserved. Printed in U.S.A.

One of the most experimental ships and cargoes that ever sailed.

Moderately bright

In the year of our Lord, eight-een hun-dred and six, we set sail from the Coal Quay of Cork, We were sail-ing a-way with a car-go of bricks for the grand Cit-y Hall in New York. We'd an el - e - gant craft, It was rigged 'fore and aft, And how the trade winds drove_____ her. She had twent - y three masts and she stood sev-'ral blasts And they called her the I-rish Rov-er.

2. There was Barney Magee from the banks of the Lee
    There was Hogan from County Tyrone
    There was Johnny McGurk who was scared stiff of work
    And a chap from Westmeath named Malone
    There was Slugger O'Toole who was drunk as a rule
    And fighting Bill Tracy from Dover
    And your man Mick McCann from the banks of the Bann
    Was the skipper on the Irish Rover.

3. We had one million bags of the best Sligo rags
    We had two million barrells of bone
    We had three million bales of old nanny goats' tails
    We had four million barrells of stone
    We had five million hogs and six million dogs
    And seven million barrells of porter
    We had eight million sides of old blind horses hides
    In the hold of the Irish Rover.

4. We had sailed seven years, when the measels broke out
    And our ship lost her way in a fog
    And the whole of the crew was reduced down to two.
    'Twas myself and the captain's old dog
    Then the ship struck a rock, O Lord what a shock
    And nearly tumbled over
    Turned nine times around then the poor old dog was drowned
    I'm the last of the Irish Rover.

ROTHSEA-O

Arranged and Adapted by LIAM CLANCY. © Copyright 1962, 1963 by TIPARM Music Publishers, Inc. International Copyright Secured. All Rights Reserved. Printed in U.S.A.

A lively party that broke up because of an attack of half-a-million fleas.

On New Year's eve in Glas-gow town When all we had was half a crown, A bunch of us thought we'd prowl a-round And find some fun in Roth - sea-o. We wan -dered out Vic-to-ri - a street, We did-n't care much for snow or sleet. And at half past two, With ach-ing feet, We found our-selves in Roth - sea - o.

CHORUS

A did-dem a do a dum a day A did-dem a do a dad-dem o. A did - dem a do a dum a day, The night we went to Roth - sea-o.

Tom Clancy here who's a bit of a lout
Said he'd treat us all to a pint of stout
So as quick as we could we all set out
For a public house in Rothsea-O.
He says, "My lads, I'd like to sing."
Says I, "You'll not do such a thing."
He says, "Clear the room and we'll make a ring
And I'll fight you all in Rothsea-O."

Chorus

Well, we had to find a place to sleep,
We were all too drunk to even creep,
We found a place that was really cheap
In a boarding house in Rothsea-O.
We all laid down to take our ease
When somebody happened for to sneeze
And he wakened half a million fleas
In a single room in Rothsea-O.

Chorus

There were several different kinds of pests,
They ran and they jumped inside our vests,
They got in our hair and they built their nests
And cried, "Hurrah for Rothsea-O."
Says I, "I think we'll head for home."
And we swore we never more would roam
And we're scratching still as we sing this poem
Of the night we spent in Rothsea-O.

JUG OF THIS

Slowly

1. Ye mourn-ers all____ as you pass by____ come in and drink____ if you are dry. Just call your drinks____ and think not a-miss____ And pop your nose____ in a jug of this.____

Ye tipplers all, if you've half a crown,
You're welcome all, for to sit down.
Just call your drinks and think not amiss
And pop your nose in a Jug of This.

When I am old, and can scarcely crow,
With an old grey beard and a head that's bald,
Crown my desire, and fulfill my wish,
A pretty young girl and a Jug of This.

When I am in my grave and dead
And all my sorrows are past and fled
Transport me then into a fish,
And let me swim, in a Jug of This.

LEWIS BRIDAL SONG

(MAIRI'S WEDDING)

Scottish Gaelic tune noted, arranged and set to English words by Hugh S. Roberton.
© Copyright 1937 by J. Curwen & Sons Ltd. London, England

CHORUS

Moderately

Step we gai - ly, On we go,

Heel for heel, and toe for toe.— Arm in arm and

on we go, All for Mair-i's wed - ding.

VERSE

Ov — er hill ways up and down

Myr - tle green and brack - en brown. Past the sheil - ing

D.C. al Fine

through the town, All for sake of Mair - i.

2. Plenty herring plenty meal
Plenty peat to fill her creel
Plenty bonny bairns as weel
That's the toast for Mairi.

(Chorus)

3. Cheeks are bright as rowans are
Brighter far than any star
Fairest of them all by far
Is my darling Mairi.

(Chorus)

4. Repeat 1st Verse

(Chorus)

OCTOBER WINDS

Arranged and Adapted by PAT CLANCY, LIAM CLANCY, TOM CLANCY, TOMMY MAKEM. © Copyright 1962, 1963 by TIPARM Music Publishers, Inc. International Copyright Secured. All Rights Reserved. Printed in U.S.A.

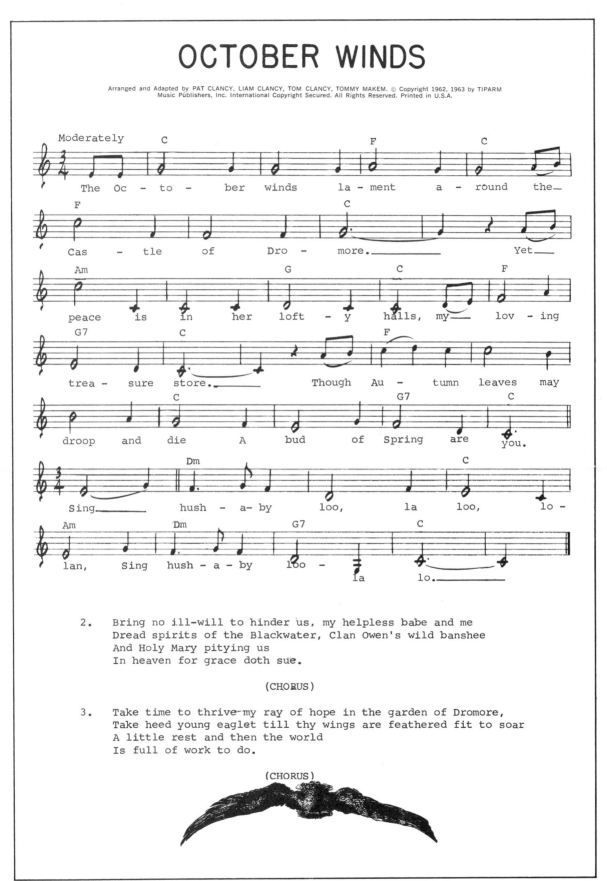

Moderately

The Oc-to-ber winds la-ment a-round the Cas-tle of Dro-more. Yet peace is in her loft-y halls, my lov-ing trea-sure store. Though Au-tumn leaves may droop and die A bud of Spring are you.

Sing hush-a-by loo, la loo, lo-lan, Sing hush-a-by loo-la lo.

2. Bring no ill-will to hinder us, my helpless babe and me
Dread spirits of the Blackwater, Clan Owen's wild banshee
And Holy Mary pitying us
In heaven for grace doth sue.

(CHORUS)

3. Take time to thrive my ray of hope in the garden of Dromore,
Take heed young eaglet till thy wings are feathered fit to soar
A little rest and then the world
Is full of work to do.

(CHORUS)

43

KEVIN BARRY

Arranged and adapted by Pat Clancy, Liam Clancy, Tom Clancy, Tommy Makem. © Copyright 1964 by Tiparm
Music Publishers Inc. International Copyright Secured. All Rights Reserved. Printed in U.S.A.

Lyric but solemn

An Irish folk tune with words from the Revolution of 1916.

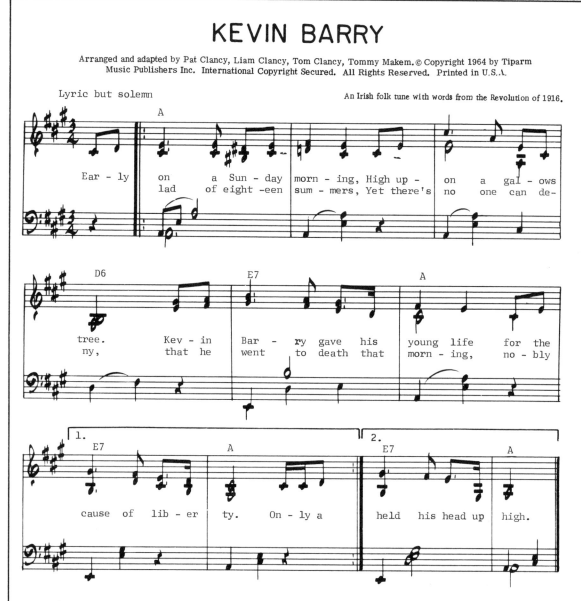

(Verse lyrics from the music:)

Ear - ly on a Sun - day morn - ing, High up - on a gal - lows tree. Kev - in Bar - ry gave his young life for the cause of lib - er - ty. On - ly a

lad of eight -een sum - mers, Yet there's no one can de- ny, that he went to death that morn - ing, no - bly held his head up high.

(CHORUS) to the same music:

"Shoot me like an Irish soldier,
Do not hang me like a dog;
For I fought for Ireland's freedom
On that dark September morn -
All around that little bakery,
Where we fought them hand to hand.
Shoot me like an Irish soldier,
For I fought to free Ireland."

Just before he faced the hangman,
In his lonely prison cell,
British soldiers tortured Barry
Just because he would not tell
All the names of his companions
Other things they wished to know;
"Turn informer, and we'll free you."
Proudly Barry answered, "no!" (CHORUS)

THE WORK OF THE WEAVERS

Arranged, Adapted and New Material by LIAM CLANCY and EWAN MacCOLL. © Copyright 1961, 1963 by TIPARM Music Publishers, Inc. International Copyright Secured. All Rights Reserved. Printed in U.S.A.

I can just see this bunch of tradesmen sitting around drinking, reassuring themselves of how the world can't get along without them.

Moderately

We're all met to-geth-er here to sit and to crack with our glass - es in our hands and our work up - on our back. There's nay a trade a - mong them that can mend or can mack, If it was -n't na for the work of the weav - - - ers.

CHORUS

If it was-n't na for the weav - ers what would ye do? You would - n't na have a cloth that's made of wool. You would - n't na have a coat of the black or the blue If it was - n't na for the work of the weav - - - ers.

There's soldiers, and there's sailors, and glaziers and all,
There's doctors, and there's ministers, and them that live by law,
And our friends in South America, though them we never saw,
But we ken they wear the work of the weavers.

(CHORUS)

The weaving's a trade that never can fail,
As long as we need clothes for to keep another hale,
So let us all be merry oh a pic'ure of good ale,
And we'll drink to the health of the weavers.

(CHORUS)

BRENNAN ON THE MOOR

Arranged, Adapted and New Material by PAT CLANCY. © Copyright 1961, 1963 by TIPARM Music Publishers, Inc. International Copyright Secured. All Rights Reserved. Printed in U.S.A.

Willie Brennan plied his trade on the Kilworth Mountains between Countys Cork and Tipperary, and was executed in Clonmel about 1846.

Fast

It's__ of a brave young highwayman, this stor-y we will tell. His name was Wil-lie Bren-nan and in Ire-land he did dwell. 'Twas on the Kil-worth moun-tains he com-menced his wild ca-reer. And man-y a wealth-y no-ble-man Be-fore him shook with fear.

CHORUS

And it's Bren-nan on the Moor, Bren-nan on the Moor, Bold__ brave and un-daunt-ed was young Bren-nan on the Moor.

One day upon the highway as Willie he went down,
He met the Mayor of Cashel a mile outside the town,
The Mayor he knew his features and he said young man, said he,
Your name is Willie Brennan, you must come along with me.

    And it's Brennan On The Moor, etc.

Now Brennan's wife had gone to town provisions for to buy,
And when she saw her Willie she commenced to weep and cry,
She said hand to me that tenpenny as soon as Willie spoke
She handed him a blunderbuss from underneath her cloak.

    For young Brennan On The Moor, etc.

Then with this loaded blunderbuss the truth I will unfold,
He made the Mayor to tremble and robbed him of his gold,
One hundred pounds was offered for his apprehension there
So he with horse and saddle to the mountains did repair.

    Did young Brennan On The Moor, etc.

Now Brennan being an outlaw upon the mountains high,
With cavalry and infantry to take him they did try,
He laughed at them with scorn until at last 'twas said
By a falsehearted woman he was cruelly betrayed.

Chorus: And it's Brennan On The Moor, etc.

I KNOW WHO IS SICK

By JOAN CLANCY and PAT CLANCY. © Copyright 1962, 1963 by TIPARM Music Publishers, Inc. International Copyright
Secured. All Rights Reserved. Printed in U.S.A.

One of our father's favorites. Only the air and first verse are his. The
rest of his song is lost.

Moderately

Am

I know who is sick, I know who is sor - ry,

G   Am

I know who I'll kiss, But the Lord knows who I'll mar - ry.

CHORUS   Am   G   Am

Too-ree-oo-ree - ay ah Too - ree-oo - ree lad - dy - o.

2.   I have stockings of silk, shoes of fine green leather,
     Combs to buckle my hair and a ring for every finger.

     (Chorus)

3.   Feather beds are soft, painted rooms are bonny,
     But I would trade them all for to go with my love Johnny.

     (Chorus)

4.   Some say he's dark, but I say he's bonny,
     Fairest of them all is my handsome, winsome Johnny.

     (Chorus)

5.   I know who is sick, I know who is sorry,
     I know who I'll kiss, but the Lord knows who I'll marry.

     (Chorus)

47

SINGIN' BIRD

This is the only love song in captivity in which the loved one is a bird.

Moderately

I have seen the lark soar__ high at morn, Heard his song__ up__ in the blue. I have heard the black-bird__ pipe his notes, The__ thrush__ and the lin - net too.

CHORUS

But there's none of them can sing so sweet, My sing - ing bird__ as__ you. Ah_____ Ah__ _____ My__ sing - ing bird as you.

2. If I could lure my singing bird
    From his own cosy nest,
    If I could catch my singing bird
    I would warm him on my breast.

    (Chorus)

3. Oh, I will climb a high, high tree
    And I'll rob a wild bird's nest
    And I'll bring back my singing bird
    To the arms that I love best.

    (Chorus)

THE LEGION OF THE REARGUARD

By J. O'Sheehan
© Copyright 1922 by J. O'Sheehan

March tempo

1. Up the Re-pub-lic, they raise their bat-tle cry,

Pearse and Mc-Der-mott will pray for you on high,

Ea - ger and read - y, for love of you they die

Proud march the sol - diers of the Rear - guard.

Chorus

Le - gion of the Rear - guard, an - swering Ire - land's call,

Hark their mar - tial tramp is heard from Cork to Don - e - gal, Wolfe

Love and Em - mett guide you, though your task be hard, De Va - le - ra

leads you, Sol - diers of the Le - gion of the Rear - guard.

Glorious the morning, through flame and shot and shell,
Now rally Ireland, your sons who love you well
Pledged, they'll defend you, through death or prison cell
Wait for the soldiers of the Rearguard.

CHORUS

Crimson the roadside, the prison wall, the cave,
Proff of their valour, go sleep in peace ye brave,
Comrade tread lightly, you're near a hero's grave,
Proud die the soldiers of the Rearguard.

CHORUS

THE MERMAID

Arranged and Adapted by PAT CLANCY, LIAM CLANCY, TOM CLANCY, TOMMY MAKEM. © Copyright 1964 by TIPARM Music Publishers, Inc. International Copyright Secured. All Rights Reserved. Printed in U.S.A.

Lively
Verse

1. It was Fri-day morn when we set sail And we were not far from the land, ____ when our cap-tain he spied a mer-maid so fair, with a comb and a glass in her hand. _____

Chorus

And the o-cean waves do roll, And the storm-y winds do blow, And we poor sail-ors are skip-ping at the top, while the land-lub-bers lie down be-low, be-low, be-low, while the land-lub-bers lie down be-low. _____

2. Then up spoke the captain of our gallant ship
   And a fine old man was he,
   "This fishy mermaid has warned me of our doom,
   We shall sink to the bottom of the sea."
   (CHORUS)

3. Then up spoke the mate of our gallant ship
   And a fine spoken man was he,
   Sayin, "I have a wife in Brooklyn by the sea
   And tonight a widow she will be."
   (CHORUS)

4. Then up spoke the cabin-boy of our gallant ship
   And a brave young lad was he,
   "Oh I have a sweetheart in Salem by the sea
   And tonight she'll be weeping for me."
   (CHORUS)

5. Then up spoke the cook of our gallant ship
   And a crazy old butcher was he,
   "I care much more for my pots and my pans
   Than I do for the bottom of the sea."
   (CHORUS)

6. Then three times 'round spun our gallant ship
   And three times 'round spun she,
   Three times 'round spun our gallant ship
   And she sank to the bottom of the sea.
   (CHORUS)

JOHNNY TODD

Arranged and Adapted by PAT CLANCY, LIAM CLANCY, TOM CLANCY, TOMMY MAKEM. © Copyright 1964 by TIPARM Music Publishers, Inc. International Copyright Secured. All rights Reserved. Printed in U.S.A.

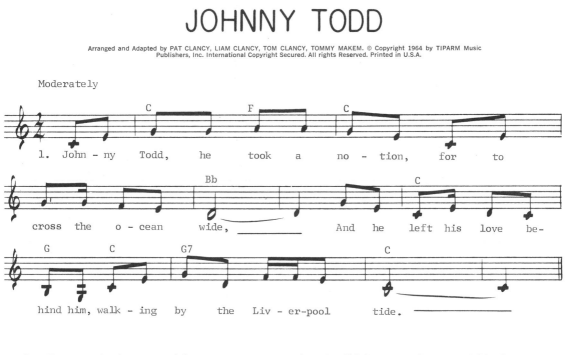

Moderately

1. John - ny Todd, he took a no - tion, for to cross the o - cean wide, _____ And he left his love be - hind him, walk - ing by the Liv - er - pool tide. _____

2. For a week she wept with sorrow,
   Tore her hair and wrung her hands,
   'Till she met another sailor
   Walking by the Liverpool sands.

3. Why fair maid are you a-weeping
   For your Johnny gone to sea,
   If you'll wed with me tomorrow
   I will kind and constant be.

4. I will buy you sheets and blankets,
   I'll buy you a wedding ring,
   You shall have a golden cradle
   For to tock the baby in.

5. Johnny Todd came home from sailing,
   Sailing on the ocean wide,
   And he found his fair and false one
   Was another sailor's bride.

6. All young men who go a-sailing
   For to fight the foreign foe,
   Do not leave your love like Johnny
   Marry her before you go.

THE JUICE OF THE BARLEY

Arranged and Adapted by LIAM CLANCY. © Copyright 1963 by TIPARM Music Publishers, Inc. International Copyright Secured.
All Rights Reserved. Printed in U.S.A.

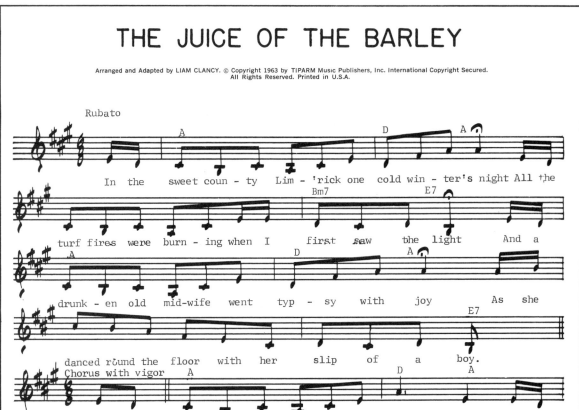

Rubato

In the sweet coun-ty Lim-'rick one cold win-ter's night All the turf fires were burn-ing when I first saw the light And a drunk-en old mid-wife went typ-sy with joy As she danced round the floor with her slip of a boy.

Chorus with vigor

Sing-ing ban-ya na mo if an gan - na, And the juice of the bar-ley for me

2. Well when I was a gossoon of eight years old or so,
With me turf and me primer to school I did to.
To a dusty old school house without any door,
Where lay the school master blind drunk on the floor.

    CHORUS

3. At the learning I wasn't such a genius I'm thinking,
But I soon bet the master entirely at drinking,
Not a wake or a wedding for five miles around,
But meself in the corner was sure to be found.

    CHORUS

4. One Sunday the priest thread me out from the altar,
Saying you'll end up your days with your neck in a halter,
And you'll dance a fine jig between heaven and hell,
And his words they did frighten me the truth for to tell.

    CHORUS

5. So the very next morning as the dawn it did break,
I went down to the vestry the pledge for to take,
And there in that room sat the priests in a bunch,
Round a big roaring fire drinking tumblers of punch.

    CHORUS

6. Well from that day to this I have wandered alone,
I'm a jack of all trades and a master of none,
With the sky for me roof and the earth for me floor,
And I'll dance out me days drinking whiskey galore.

CHORUS

THE JUG OF PUNCH

By FRANCIS McPEAKE. (Based on a traditional theme.) Arranged by Peter Kennedy. © Copyright 1960 by ESSEX Music, Ltd., London, England. All publication rights controlled by HOLLIS Music, Inc., New York, N. Y., for the U.S.A. and by ESSEX Music of Canada, Ltd., Toronto, for Canada.

Verse

As I was sit-tin' with jug and spoon on one fine morn in the month of June, A bird-ie sat on an i-vy bunch, And the song he sang was the Jug of Punch.

Chorus

Too-ra Loo-ra loo, Too-ra Loo-ra loo, Too-ra Loo-ra loo, Too-ra Loo-ra loo. A bird-ie sat on an i-vy bunch, And the song he sang was the Jug of Punch.

What more diversion can a man desire
Than to court a girl by a neat turf fire
With a kerry pippin to crack an' crunch
Aye, an' on the table a jug of punch.

The learned doctors with all their art
Cannot cure the impression that's on the heart
Even the cripple forgets his hunch
When he's safe outside of a jug of punch.

And when I'm dead and in my grave
No costly tombstone will I crave
Just lay me down in my native peat
With a jug of punch at my head and feet.

THE LEAVING OF LIVERPOOL

Arranged and adapted with new words by Pat Clancy, Liam Clancy, Tom Clancy, Tommy Makem. Copyright

Moderately
Verse

1. Fare - well to you, my own true love, I am
go - ing far a - way. I am
bound for Cal - i - for - ni - a, but I
know that I'll re - turn some day.

Chorus

So fare thee well, my own true love, and when
I re - turn, u - nit - ed we will be. It's not the
leav - ing of Liv - er - pool that grieves me, but my
dar - ling, when I think of thee.

2. I have shipped on a Yankee sailing ship,
Davy Crockett is her name,
And Burgess is the captain of her
And they say she is a floating hell.
(CHORUS)

3. Oh the sun is on the harbour love,
And I wish I could remain,
For I know it will be some long time
Before I see you again.
(CHORUS)

54

THE COBBLER

New Words, Arranged and Adapted by TOMMY MAKEM. © Copyright 1962, 1963 by TIPARM Music Publishers, Inc. International Copyright Secured. All Rights Reserved. Printed in U.S.A.

Oh me name is Dick Dar - by, I'm a cob - bler, I ser - ved me time at old camp. Some call me an old ag - i - ta - tor, But now I'm re - solved to re - pent.

Chorus

With me ing - twing of an ing - thing of an i - day, with me ing-twing of an ing-thing of an i - day, with me roo-boo- boo - roo - boo-boo ran - dy, and me lab stone keeps beat - ing a - way.

Now my father was hung for sheep-stealing,
Me mother was burned for a witch,
My sister's a dandy housekeeper,
And I'm a mechanical switch. (Chorus)

Ah, it's forty long years I have traveled,
All by the contents of me pack,
Me hammers, me awls and me pinches,
I carry them all on me back. (Chorus)

Oh, my wife she is humpy, she's lumpy,
My wife she's the devil, she's black,
And no matter what I may do with her
Her tongue it goes clickety-clack. (Chorus)

It was early one fine summer's morning,
A little before it was day,
I dipped her three times in the river,
And carelessly bade her "Good day!"

THE VALLEY OF KNOCKANURE

Arranged and Adapted by LIAM CLANCY. © Copyrighted 1963 by TIPARM Music Publishers, Inc. International Copyright Secured. All Rights Reserved. Printed in U.S.A.

This action occurred in the "Black and Tan" war in 1921.

Rubato

1. You may sing or speak a-bout East-er week or the he-roes of nine-ty eight Those Fen - ian men who roamed the glen for vic - try or de - feat Their names on his - to - ry's page are told, their mem - o - ries will en - dure Not a song was sung a-bout three young men in the Val-ley of Knok- a - nure.

2. There was Lyons and Walsh and the Dalton boy, they were young and in their prime
They rambled to a lonely spot where the Black and Tans did hide
The Republic bold they did uphold, tho' outlawed on the moor
And side by side they fought and died in the Valley of Knockanure.

3. It was on a neighbouring hillside we listened in hushed dismay
In every house, in every town a young girl knelt to pray
They're closing in around them now with rifle fire so sure
And Lyons is dead and young Dalton's down in the Valley of Knockanure.

4. But e'er the guns could seal his fate, young Walsh had broken thro'
With a prayer to God he spurned the sod as against the hill he flew
The bullets tore his flesh in two yet he cried with voice so sure,
"Revenge I'll get for my comrade's death in the Valley of Knockanure."

5. The summer sun is sinking low behind the field and lea
The pale moon light is shining bright far off beyond Tralee
The dismal stars and the clouds afar are darkening o'er the moor
And the Banshee cried when young Dalton died in the Valley of Knockanure

AHEM, AHEM

With spirit   In recitative style - the notes represent approximate pitches.

A - hem, a - hem, me moth - er is gone to church,___ She told me not to play with you be-cause you're in the dirt.___ It is - n't be - cause you're dirt - y, It is - n't be - cause you're clean, It's be - cause you have the whoop - ing cough and eat mar - gar - ine.___

57

FARE THEE WELL ENNISKILLEN

Music: Traditional. New Words by TOMMY MAKEM.

Lively tempo

Verse

1. Our troop was made read-y at the dawn of the day From love-ly En-nis-kil-len they were march-ing us a-way They put us then on board a ship to cross the rag-ing main To fight in blood-y bat-tle in the sun-ny land of Spain.

Chorus

Fare thee well En-nis-kil-len, fare thee well for a while And all a-round the bor-ders of Er-in's green isle And when the war is o-ver we'll re-turn in full bloom And you'll all wel-come home the En-nis-kil-len Drag-oons.

Oh Spain it is a gallant land where wine and ale flow free
There's lots of lovely women there to dandle on your knee
And often in a tavern there we'd make the rafters ring
When every soldier in the house would raise his glass and sing.
(CHORUS)

Well we fought for Ireland's glory there and many a man did fall,
From musket and from bayonet and from thundering cannon ball
And many a foeman we laid low, amid the battle throng,
And as we prepared for action you would often hear this song.
(CHORUS)

Well now the fighting's over and for home we have set sail
Our flag above this lofty ship is fluttering in the gale
They've given us a pension boys of fourpence each a day
And when we reach Enniskillen never more we'll have to say.
(CHORUS)

SHOALS OF HERRING

Words and Music by EWAN MacCOLL. © Copyright 1962, 1963 by STORMKING Music, Inc.
International Copyright Secured. All Rights Reserved. Printed in U.S.A.

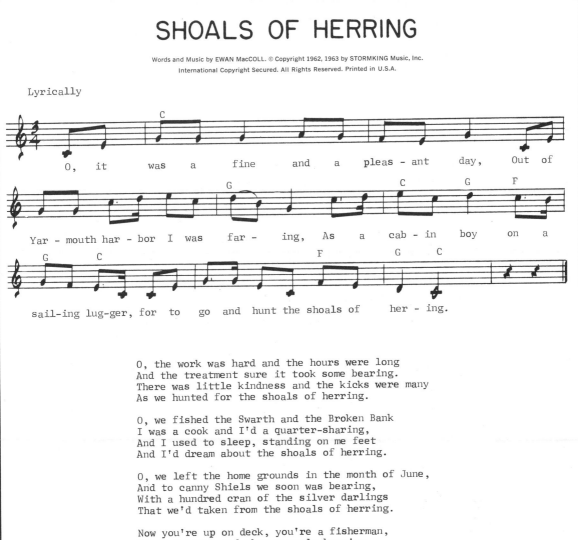

Lyrically

O, it was a fine and a pleas-ant day, Out of Yar-mouth har-bor I was far-ing, As a cab-in boy on a sail-ing lug-ger, for to go and hunt the shoals of her-ing.

O, the work was hard and the hours were long
And the treatment sure it took some bearing.
There was little kindness and the kicks were many
As we hunted for the shoals of herring.

O, we fished the Swarth and the Broken Bank
I was a cook and I'd a quarter-sharing,
And I used to sleep, standing on me feet
And I'd dream about the shoals of herring.

O, we left the home grounds in the month of June,
And to canny Shiels we soon was bearing,
With a hundred cran of the silver darlings
That we'd taken from the shoals of herring.

Now you're up on deck, you're a fisherman,
You can swear and show a manly bearing,
Take your turn on watch with the other fellows
While you're searching for the shoals of herring.

In the stormy seas and the living gales
Just to earn your daily bread you're daring,
From the Dover Straits to the Faroe Islands
As you're following the shoals of herring.

O, I earned me keep and I paid me way,
And I earned the gear that I was wearing,
Sailed a million miles, caught ten-million fishes
We were sailing after shoals of herring.

THE GALLANT FORTY TWA

Arranged and Adapted by DAVID HAMMOND, PAT CLANCY, LIAM CLANCY, TOM CLANCY, TOMMY MAKEM. © Copyright 1964 by TIPARM Music Publishers, Inc. International Copyright Secured. All Rights Reserved. Printed in U.S.A.

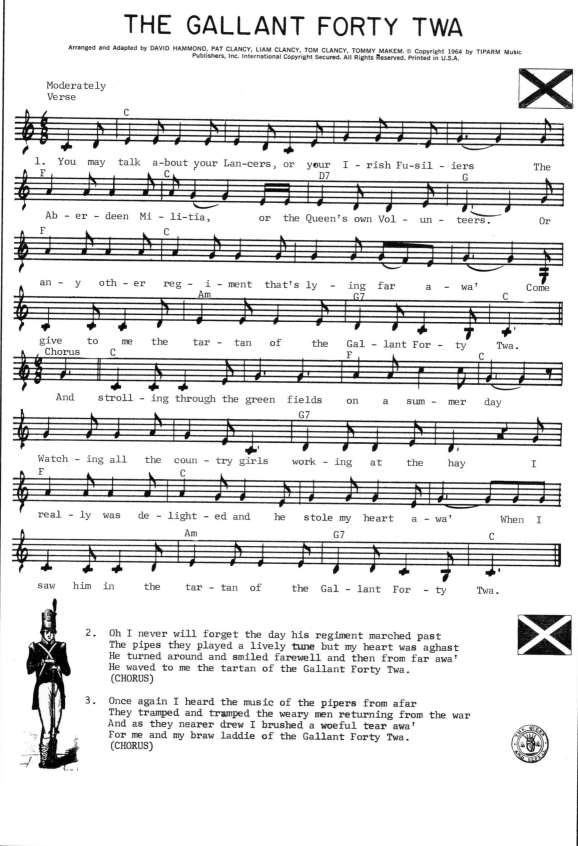

Moderately
Verse

1. You may talk a-bout your Lan-cers, or your I-rish Fu-sil-iers The Ab-er-deen Mi-li-tia, or the Queen's own Vol-un-teers. Or an-y oth-er reg-i-ment that's ly-ing far a-wa' Come give to me the tar-tan of the Gal-lant For-ty Twa.

Chorus

And stroll-ing through the green fields on a sum-mer day Watch-ing all the coun-try girls work-ing at the hay I real-ly was de-light-ed and he stole my heart a-wa' When I saw him in the tar-tan of the Gal-lant For-ty Twa.

2. Oh I never will forget the day his regiment marched past
The pipes they played a lively tune but my heart was aghast
He turned around and smiled farewell and then from far awa'
He waved to me the tartan of the Gallant Forty Twa.
(CHORUS)

3. Once again I heard the music of the pipers from afar
They tramped and tramped the weary men returning from the war
And as they nearer drew I brushed a woeful tear awa'
For me and my braw laddie of the Gallant Forty Twa.
(CHORUS)

ROW BULLIES ROW

Arranged and adapted by Pat Clancy, Tom Clancy, Liam Clancy, Tommy Makem. © Copyright 1964 by Tiparm
Music Publishers Inc. International Copyright Secured. All Rights Reserved. Printed in U.S.A.

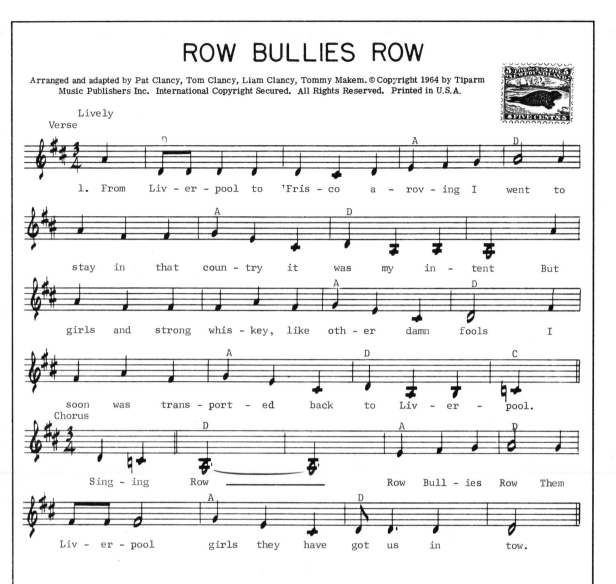

Lively

Verse

1. From Liv-er-pool to 'Fris-co a-rov-ing I went to stay in that coun-try it was my in-tent But girls and strong whis-key, like oth-er damn fools I soon was trans-port-ed back to Liv-er-pool.

Chorus

Sing-ing Row _____ Row Bull-ies Row Them Liv-er-pool girls they have got us in tow.

2. We shipped on the "Alaska" lying out in the bay
   Awaiting for a fair wind to get under way
   The sailors all drunk and their backs is all sore
   Their whiskey's all gone and they can't get no more.
   (CHORUS)

3. I remember one day we were crossing the line
   When I think on it now, sure we had a good time
   She was driving bows under, the sailors all wet
   She was doing twelve knots, with the main sky sail set.
   (CHORUS)

4. And now we've arrived at the Bramleymore dock
   All the fair maids and lassies around us do flock.
   Our whiskey's all gone and our six quid advance
   And I think it's high time for to get up and dance.
   (CHORUS)

CARRICKFERGUS

Arranged and Adapted by PAT CLANCY, LIAM CLANCY, TOM CLANCY, TOMMY MAKEM. © Copyright 1964 by TIPARM Music Publishers, Inc. International Copyright Secured. All rights Reserved. Printed in U.S.A.

Very freely

1. I wish I was _____ in Car-rick-fer-gus on-ly for nights _____ in Bal-ly-grand I would swim o-ver _____ the deep-est o-cean on-ly for nights _____ in Bal-ly grand. Ah but the sea is wide _____ and I can-not swim o-ver, _____ nor have I wings _____ so I could fly I wish I could meet _____ a hand-some boat-man ___ to fer-ry me o-ver to my love and die.

2. But in Kilkenny it is reported
   They have marble stones there as black as ink,
   With gold and silver, I did support her,
   But I'll sing no more, till I get a drink.
   I'm drunk today and I'm seldom sober,
   A handsome rover from town to town,
   Ah but I'm sick now, my days are numbered,
   Come all you young men and I'll lay me down.

BONNY CHARLIE

Arranged and Adapted by PAT CLANCY, LIAM CLANCY, TOM CLANCY, TOMMY MAKEM. © Copyright 1964 by TIPARM Music
Publishers, Inc. International Copyright Secured. All Rights Reserved. Printed in U.S.A.

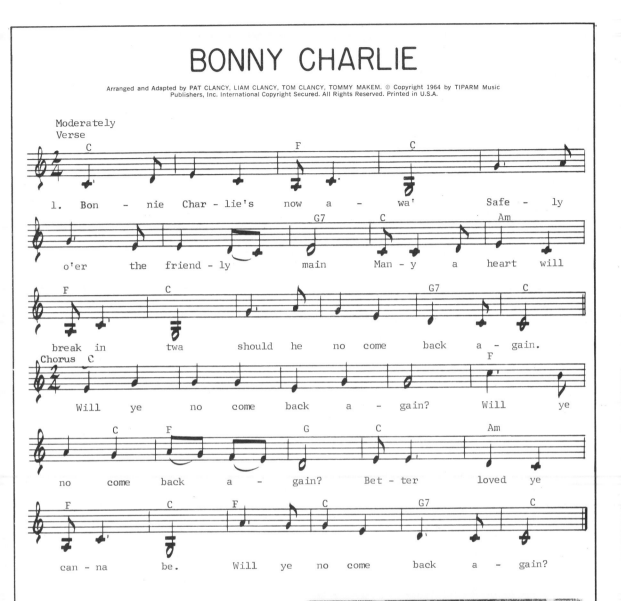

Moderately
Verse

1. Bon - nie Char - lie's now a - wa' Safe - ly o'er the friend - ly main Man - y a heart will break in twa should he no come back a - gain.

Chorus

Will ye no come back a - gain? Will ye no come back a - gain? Bet - ter loved ye can - na be. Will ye no come back a - gain?

2. Whene're I hear the blackbird sing
Unto the evening sinking down
Or thrush that makes the woods to ring
To me there is no other sound.
(CHORUS)

3. Many a gallant soldier fought
Many a gallant chief did fall
Death itself was dearly bought
All for Scotland's King and Lord.
(CHORUS)

4. Low the blackbird's note and long
Lilting wildly up the glen
And aye to me he sings one song
Will ye no come back again?
(CHORUS)

THE PARTING GLASS

Arranged and adapted by Liam Clancy and Tommy Makem. © Copyright 1961 by Tiparm Music Publishers Inc.
International Copyright Secured. All Rights Reserved. Printed in U.S.A.

The traditional farewell song of the Clancy family.

Very rubato

O___ all the mon-ey that e'er I spent, I___ spent it in good___ com-pa-ny And___ all the harm___ that e'er I've done, a - las, it was___ to___ none but me. And all___ I've___ done for want___ of___ wit to mem-'ry now I___ can't re-call. So___ fill to me___ the part-ing glass good-night, and joy___ be___ with you all.

2. O all the comrades that e'er I had are sorry for my going away
    And all the sweethearts that e'er I had would wish me one more
        day to stay
    But since it falls into my lot that I should rise and you should not,
    I'll gently rise and softly call, goodnight, and joy be with you all.